HANDBOOKS OF EUROPEAN NATIONAL DANCES

EDITED BY
VIOLET ALFORD

DANCES OF HUNGARY

Plate 1
'Matyó' national costume

DANCES of HUNGARY

GEORGE BUDAY

NOVERRE PRESS

ILLUSTRATED BY
GEORGE BUDAY, A.R.E.
ASSISTANT EDITOR
YVONNE MOYSE

First published in 1950
This edition published in 2021 by
The Noverre Press
Southwold House
Isington Road
Binsted
Hampshire
GU34 4PH

ISBN 978-1-914311-03-1

© 2021 The Noverre Press

CONTENTS

INTRODUCTION	Page 7
The Hajdutánc	8
Recruiting Dances	9
The Csárdás	10
A Wedding	11
Survivals of Ritual Dances	15
Work Dances and Dance-Games	15
Village Dance Etiquette	16
Music	17
Costume	18
When Dancing May Be Seen	20
Centres of Folk Dance, etc.	21
THE DANCES	22
Poise of Body and Arm Gestures	23
Basic Steps	23
Csárdás Steps	24
Palóc Mártogatós vagy Kukorgós	27
Kalotaszegi Forgós	30
Kunszentmiklósi Verbunkos	32
Karádi Bebug-Verbunk	36
NOTE ON PRONUNCIATION	38
BIBLIOGRAPHY	40

Illustrations in Colour, pages 2, 12, 29, 39
Map of Hungary, page 6

INTRODUCTION

THE Magyar ancestors of the Hungarian people came into Europe about the end of the ninth century. One of the earliest references to dancing is by the monk of St. Gall, the Chronicler Ekkehard, who describes Hungarian soldiers who fought near Lake Constance as dancing 'jubilant with joy' before their leaders; after which we hear little till 1470, when King Matthias Corvinus himself footed a Hungarian dance for the Emperor, and again when his bride, Beatrice of Aragon, was shown dancing 'in the Hungarian manner'. In the seventeenth century dances such as the Pavane, Galliard and Courante were welcomed at Court and in the great houses as in other European countries, and in the eighteenth century the Contredanse type developed a Hungarian form. One old Court dance was Palotás, the Palace dance, in which even the clergy took part holding the end of a handkerchief instead of the hand of their partners. Besides Court dances it was always customary to include folk dances at the balls of the aristocracy, who then wore genuine peasant costumes.

Hungary, like other countries, from early times suffered disapproval of dancing. Familiar medieval decrees of the Church forbade dancing and gaiety; the Erdy MS. for example tells us of the ban in 1038 on any but church musical instruments and on dancing after the death of St. Stephen, while the Synod of Buda, 1279, warned the

clergy against any tolerance of dancing in churchyards—
which sometimes meant in the churches themselves.
Later a Synod of the Reformed church forbade any of
its officials to dance. Yet, as elsewhere, none of these
could suppress the dancing habits of the people.

THE HAJDUTÁNC

The best-known and most popular dance in the sixteenth
and seventeenth centuries was perhaps the Hajdutánc.
Between 1514 and 1651 it was described many times,
and appears also in a German MS. of about 1592 as
Heiducken Dantz. An English traveller, Edward Brown,
'M.D. of the College of London, Physician in Ordinary
to His Majesty' (Charles II) saw it in 1669 danced with
naked swords '... clashing the same, turning, winding,
elevating and depressing their bodies with strong and
active motions ... singing withal unto their measures'.
This—the usual sort of traveller's tale—does not allow
us to know for certain whether the Hajdutánc was a true
Hilt and Point sword dance, though the 'winding' and
that it was a peasant not a Guild dance incline one to
think so. This we learn from records of the great peasant
revolution in 1514, learning also of the shocking end of
the revolutionary leader, burnt to death by the barbaric
nobles who forced his comrades to dance the Hajdutánc
round their dying chief.

This dance survives in part in the various Stick dances,
Botos-tánc, such as the Shepherds' and Swineherds'
dances, the sword replaced by a stick or an axe. But it
has now taken the well-known English Bacca Pipes form,
two sticks laid on the ground with steps over them and
in the angles. There is also a Couple stick dance of quite
other signification, the Botoló dance of Porcsalma, in which
the stick apparently symbolises the power of the man
over the woman. This symbol is found again in the

wedding feast when the young husband is ceremoniously presented with a stick, while in some Transdanubian wedding dances—the Mozsártánc for example—the stick is unmistakably a phallic symbol.

RECRUITING DANCES

The French wars of the eighteenth century necessitated vigorous recruiting campaigns, an important part of which was choreographical. At this time emerge the various male dances called Verbunkós (or Verbunk), first described in the 1770's. Between this date and 1848 recruiting commissions, consisting of a handful of hussars with their sergeant and corporal, invaded the villages, chose a suitable spot, hoisted a flag and forming a circle began their dance. This consisted of slow figures alternating with short quick ones. In the middle of the circle the corporal directed the dancing and drinking while the sergeant acted as Master of Ceremonies. Those village lads who decided to enlist went into the circle and the merry-making would go on for hours, repeated for days, until the required number of recruits was obtained. The story goes that in one day in 1840 in the town of Szeged, thirteen hundred young men were thus enticed into the army.

By 1790 the chief characteristics of the Verbunkós were already developed. Its violin accompaniment gave the alternation of slow and quick movements, later called hallgató and friss parts, the staccato rhythm emphasised by boots and spurs; ankle-knocking (bokázás), hand-clapping and heel-clicking with definite major or minor melodies had all by then taken shape. The present more stylised composition is however from the 1830's only. The music is always based on a folk-song with its text. The Verbunks of Kóny and Kunszentmiklós are the best-known today.

The national introduction of the Verbunk coincided with the revival of national literature and aspirations, and soon Hungarian musicians were composing music for it, while foreign composers such as Haydn, Beethoven, Berlioz and Brahms fell captive to its rhythm. It became one of the sources of national opera and ballet, and in the hands of Mosonyi and Liszt forms the basis of Hungary's modern symphonic music. Even Bartók's first compositions inherited much from its music, and mention should be made of Kodály's and Sándor Veress's beautiful Verbunks.

The Verbunkós was used as the opening dance at aristocratic balls, while the people continued to dance it on solemn occasions such as the initiation of young lads into the adult age-group and the great pig-killing feasts.

THE CSÁRDÁS

Csárdás means 'inn dance', and was thus called by the aristocracy who identified it with 'what is danced by the daughters of the serfs in the lowest inns on Sundays'. It is a stylised, simplified form of elements from the Verbunkós—the quick movement of which had already been called Csárdás—together with a Couple dance, the Vegyes páros. Although disdained, it swept through the ball-rooms of the nobility at the same time as the Körmagyar, a nineteenth-century composed figure dance, and went back to the people who, however, did not call it by the derogatory name. Its popularity presently gave it the position of 'the Hungarian national dance' about 1839, when it was witnessed by another English traveller, John Paget, Esq., at Füred. 'We had an opportunity this evening of seeing the Hungarian National dance very well performed. . . . The dance becomes quicker and quicker as it goes on', he says, 'till at last the gentleman seizes his partner in his arms, whirls her round and round, quits her, again seizes her and at last conducts her to a seat quite exhausted. . . . To me it seems the most pantomimic of any dance I know [he could never have seen the Italian Saltarello]; it is impossible not to see the courtship of the lover, the coy reserve of the maiden, the gradual yielding and the final triumph of love . . .' He finishes by mildly remarking, ' I cannot say it is an elegant dance; but it is full of expression and requires no small agility to perform it well '.

A WEDDING

As in most peasant communities, this is the great occasion for music and dance. Hungarian marriage ceremonies begin at the betrothal, which contains survivals from the ' buying the bride' custom already fully described as early as 1050. The groom and his friends arrive at the bride's house in the evening and are admitted with difficulty. They are offered the eldest woman dressed up like a young girl, or three veiled women to choose from. After the discovery of the real bride blessings and drinking follow and the exchange of a coin hidden in flowers—and with this the girl is 'sold'. A dinner ends the betrothal ceremonies, the young couple eating from the same dish and drinking from the same glass. Then the dancing begins and goes on till morning.

The whole proceedings, which continue for two or three days, are threaded on dancing. The kendöfa (literally: kerchief tree) is set up in front of both houses, that before the young man's home decorated with farm tools, that before the girl's with women's things, brooms and kitchen utensils. All this is accompanied by dancing and singing.

The conveying of the nuptial bed to the new house makes another occasion for song as it is paraded on a wagon up and down the village street, the day before the ceremony, piled with new bedding. When it at last

Plate 2
Kunszentmiklós

arrives and is made up, the party catches a little boy and throws him on the immense pile of eiderdowns—sympathetic magic—that the first child may be a son. Then everybody dances the Bedmakers' dance. In the Nógrád region the women dance a pillow dance, the pillow held high above their heads, others carrying the eiderdown. They make a beautiful sight, turning and bending, the pillows waving rhythmically in the air. Special songs accompany the bed to its home, one of which runs:

> *They're carrying the bed of the bride,*
> *The bridegroom's place of rest.*
> *Let God give it His blessing.*
> *In a year's time a pretty lassie,*
> *In a year's time a pretty lassie!*

The singers of this song evidently, like Sally Waters, prefer a girl as first-born—

> *Now you're married we wish you joy:*
> *First a girl and then a boy . . .*

While the betrothal rites descend from the old purchase of the bride, the marriage ceremonies signify her handing-over by her family. On the great morning groups set out to collect the invited guests. They dance and bid farewell to the bridegroom's single life before going with music to the house of the bride, the gate of which is barricaded by a rope.

Inside, the bridesmaids are dressing the bride who may not raise a finger to help herself, before she dances the Farewell dance, Búcsú-tánc, with the best man. Floods of tears are expected from the bride, who kisses her family repeatedly as though she would never see them again. Then the best man with his decorated stick gives the signal, the musicians strike up, and the procession starts. Shouting, shooting and the breaking of crockery accompany the march—originally to frighten away evil influences. Sometimes there is a dance, Paptánc, the Priests' dance, in front of, or even in, the church, probably a survival of the dancing in churchyards so reprobated in the Middle Ages. And dancing they return after the marriage service.

Strict custom rules the midday meal taken in the two family houses, after which the bride is fetched with a ' flag ' and the Stáció dance *en route*. She is lifted from the carriage (a parallel to the Indo-European lifting over the threshold), wheat is thrown at her (fertility magic), and she sometimes has to dance three times round a fire before entering the house, where the mother-in-law receives her.

The evening feast often begins with the Becsülettánc, the Dance of Honour, later masked or fur-covered ' Turks ' appear to dance with the bride,* but at last comes the ritual fektetés, or putting to bed, about midnight. The first act is a dance with the exhausted bride by every man present who gives her money for it, then, in some places, Kendötánc, the Kerchief dance, each partner putting a shawl round the bride's shoulders, whereupon enters the vöfély, an important marriage functionary, bearing three lighted candles between the fingers of his left hand, who takes the bride on his arm. He speechifies about marriage, blowing the candles out one by one, and runs with the bride out of the room. In some districts women accompany her to the bridal room in slow procession with mournful music, the young men doing the same for the groom. The vöfély lifts the bridal crown from the bride's head with his stick, and the company dances nine times round the house as a final magical act.

The next day the married woman's cap is placed on the bride's head and another procession takes the party

* This is powerful fertility magic and in Scandinavian countries is done by ' Bears ', also fur-clad.—*Editor*.

to the village square, where they light a bonfire, dance round it and the bride jumps over it several times as a safeguard against being bewitched. Many other ceremonies and dances inherited from primitive times may be carried out.

SURVIVALS OF RITUAL DANCES

Funeral dances have survived almost to the present time. Announcement of her husband's death was made quite recently by a woman with wailing cries and rhythmic arm-waving which suggest the memory of ancient mourning rites. The funeral feast often ended with a dance, especially when the dead man was young and unmarried, when his ' wedding ceremony ' was symbolised by a dance round the grave. During a recent funeral feast in the farm lands round Szeged, the hired mourners—women like the Pyrenean *pleureuses*—danced with wine flasks on their heads.

Remnants of ancient ritual survive also in the regös, or minstrels' performances (Transylvania and Transdanubia), at the time of the winter solstice, and in the nation-wide Bethlehem-járás at Christmas, the carrying-round of the crib with dances by the impersonators of the Bethlehem shepherds.

There are, of course, the seasonal festivals of May Day with its maypole, Májusfa, the Whitsuntide activities, harvest and vintage feasts and the jumping through the flames of the St. John's Eve fire.

WORK DANCES AND DANCE-GAMES

Craftsmen often possess their own peculiar dance and in Hungary we can show the Weavers' dance, Takácstánc, in which the dancers cleverly imitate the passing of the shuttle on a loom by rhythmically pushing through and picking up a hat between their legs. At the vintage the coopers of the famous Tokay wine district solemnly perform their annual Bodnártánc, Coopers' dance, portraying their own work. The reapers' dance, Kaszástánc, is symbolic and at the same time erotic. Under this heading may perhaps come the ancient Rumanian Girl's dance by a male solo dancer miming the story of the goat, lost and recovered by the shepherdess.

Although children's games and dance-games naturally take a ring formation, the great circular Kolo, so popular in the Balkans, is hardly known in Hungary. We must mention the Sheep, Mouse, Wolf and Cat dance-games, the Chicken, Cushion, Clap dances, the Duck dance of Okány, and the revived Kállai Kettös dance (couple dance of Kálló).

VILLAGE DANCE ETIQUETTE

In old days, and to a lesser extent today, the communal spinning-rooms were the meeting-places of young men and girls, and the long evenings spent in them were the special occasions for flirtation and courting, which always ended with games and dancing. Other occasions are pilgrimages, fairs, soldiers' balls held in the autumn, and dances after the initiation of the lads, at the pig-killing feasts and at all family and social gatherings. Following the manifold divisions which emerged in rural society in modern times there were separate balls for the rich, or 'fattened' (zsiros), peasants—the kuláks—and for the poorer peasants, farm labourers, shepherds and so on. Even the gypsies, who are the village musicians, have their own balls, and dance to barrel organs so that none that night need play the music.

The usual places for dancing are the house, barn or yard. When a new barn is built a csürdöngölö dance is given to help level the earthen floor. People dance in inns and village squares, and at carnival time 'dancing-rooms' are hired for married and unmarried couples separately.

Dances begin with the bemuzsikálás, music to warm up the company. The men will usually begin to dance by themselves and later, by a wink or calling a name, 'pull in' the girls. Sometimes one of them is caught round the waist and literally pulled into the dance. A young man, called legénybiró or 'first lad', with assistants keeps order during a ball. The girls are invited by young men who pay their entry for them, and who have to fetch them and escort them home again. The etiquette at these balls is very strict. If a girl needlessly offends a young man, or refuses to dance with him but accepts another, note is taken of the offence. At the next ball the slighted partner stands forth, the gypsy fiddlers are commanded to play the 'marching-out' tune and the girl goes out followed by her family, all weeping. Or, still more drastically, the men, during the Hopszapolka, drive the dance towards the door. This is suddenly flung open and out goes the culprit, literally rolled out on the floor.

MUSIC

'Mon intention était', wrote the great composer Franz Liszt in 1838, 'de m'enfoncer seul, à pied, le sac sur le dos, dans les parties les plus désertes de la Hongrie. Il n'en fut point ainsi.' If he had done so the real folk music of Hungary might have been discovered a century earlier.

The music most popular amongst Hungarians and best known to foreigners is the string orchestra of gypsy musicians. The first record of these wandering players in Hungary comes to us from 1489, and gradually their name, Cigány, became identified with their profession, so that in the eighteenth and nineteenth centuries they were considered the exclusive executants of Hungarian

folk music. But—exactly as happened in southern Spain—
they interpreted it in their own way and have been responsible for a deep change in the soul of the country's inherited music and dance traditions. The Hungarian composers Béla Bartók and Zoltán Kodály, searching for the true Magyar inheritance and its developments—largely pentatonic—have had to rediscover them by separating them from the all-pervading gypsy-influenced overlay.

The gypsy is past master of the violin, but the cimbalom is his also. This is of the dulcimer family, trapeziform, metal-stringed, and is an essential part of a gypsy band. The player lays it on a table or on his knees, when it is held in place by a strap round his neck.

Other folk instruments with a long ancestry—some of them now obsolete—are the kürt (ox-horn), the duda (bagpipe), the forgólant or tekerölant, related to the vielle, the furulya (a shepherd's willow flute) and the tárogató, an instrument with historical associations connected with the Rákóczi revolution. So dear is and was this instrument to the people that some generations later, in the 1790's, its peculiar sound created such excitement amongst the population of a garrison town in the Alföld that they took to arms and drove out the occupying Austrian troops.

COSTUME

Hungary's wonderful treasury of costume is too rich even to be summarised, but since the dress may be said to dance with the men and women who wear it, a few remarks here will complement the picture given by the illustrations of particular costumes. Contemporary Hungarian dances are meant to be performed in top boots, spurred for the man, and of great significance in the dance. Hats, often decorated with flowers, feathers or ribbons, are worn, to be snatched off and waved. The woman's silk head-kerchief answers the same purpose, is used as a link between her and her partner and more prosaically for mopping her face.

Male dress shows two types, tight-fitting trousers or the gatya, the skirt-like wide linen breeches, and the dancer's rhythm and movement will vary according to which he wears. The woman swings her many petticoats and the kerchiefs attached to her hip or her hair, while small cushions or rolled-up towels pad her form to exaggerate its contours—yet facial make-up is considered most immoral. Many small charms are performed before balls. A girl will put magical frankincense into her top boots, or weave into her skirt a bit of violin string which was broken at a wedding when the Bridal dance was being played—the first to secure plenty of partners, the second to make sure of getting a husband.

The Csárdás, having now emerged as a national dance, may be performed in any regional costumes without offending local pride.

The author wishes to express his sincere thanks to Mme Zsuzsa Ortutay, President of the Hungarian Folk Dance Association, and to Dr. István Tálasi, of the Ethnological Institute, Budapest, for their kind help in providing valuable source-material. He is also indebted to Mlle Emma Lugossy and M. Ferenc Béres, of the Budapest Ethnographical Museum, who supplied the dance tunes.

July 31st, 1949   G. B.

OCCASIONS WHEN DANCING MAY BE SEEN

Amongst the dance-loving Hungarian people fêtes are too numerous to be recorded other than the following:

All the great calendar festivals.

May 1st.

The Day of the New Bread, August 20th, which is rapidly replacing the festivities in honour of St. Stephen on that day. Thousands of villagers in traditional costume come into Budapest to celebrate the harvest.

Weddings.

Carnival.

CENTRES OF FOLK DANCE, FOLK MUSIC AND FOLKLORE STUDY

For all scholarly, artistic, educational and social enquiries: The Hungarian Folk Dance Association, Magyar Táncszövetség, Bajza-u. 26, Budapest VI.

Recording, analysis and study, films of village dancing: The Ethnological Department of the East European Institute, Keleteurópai Intézet Néptudományi Intézete, Esterházy-u. 28, Budapest VIII.

Dance College: Tánc- és Kóruskollégium, Siófok, Veszprém megye.

Folk Music Section, Budapest Ethnographical Museum, Néprajzi Múzeum, Könyves Kálmán-krt. 40, Budapest X.

Folk dance performances arranged by the 'Bouquet Society', Bokréta Szövetség, Felhö-u. 3, Budapest XII.

Folk dances are taught at the Siófok Peasant High School: Paraszt-föiskola, Siófok, Veszprém megye.

THE DANCES

TECHNICAL EDITORS
MURIEL WEBSTER AND KATHLEEN P. TUCK

ABBREVIATIONS
USED IN DESCRIPTION OF STEPS AND DANCES

r—right ⎱ referring to R—right ⎱ describing turns or
l—left ⎰ hand, foot, etc. L—left ⎰ ground pattern
C—clockwise C-C—counter-clockwise

For descriptions of foot positions and explanations of any ballet terms the following books are suggested for reference:

A Primer of Classical Ballet (Cecchetti method). Cyril Beaumont.

First Steps (R.A.D.). Ruth French and Felix Demery.

The Ballet Lover's Pocket Book. Kay Ambrose.

Reference books for description of figures:

The Scottish Country Dance Society's Publications. Many volumes, from Thornhill, Cairnmuir Road, Edinburgh 12.

The English Folk Dance and Song Society's Publications. Cecil Sharp House, 2 Regent's Park Road, London, N.W.1.

The Country Dance Book I–VI. Cecil J. Sharp. Novello & Co., London.

POISE OF BODY AND ARM GESTURES

Both men and women have a proud and upright bearing, the men an almost stiff poise from the waist upwards.

In solo dances, the man often holds his hands high above his head or sideways at shoulder-level. Both hands or one hand behind the back, palm outward, is very typical although hands on the hips is also commonly used.

The women have a great variety of hand gestures, the most usual one being hands on hips, palms outward. The hands (either both or one) are sometimes held behind the head.

In couple dances, the most usual grasp is man's hands on woman's waist, her hands resting on his shoulders. Hand grasp is also used and also elbow grasp, the characteristic feature of all being that the man must have full control of his partner's movements. She obeys his every dictate and whirls and turns as he wills.

BASIC STEPS

The dances are very spontaneous and the steps cannot be strictly defined except in their basic form. The elaborations and ornamentations of the simple basic steps provide rich material for the skilled dancer. The inner rhythm or pulse of the step is more important than the actual pattern, and this cannot be set down but must be felt.

Under each notated dance, the steps peculiar to that dance are described. As the Csárdás is not given in dance form, a few examples of simple Csárdás steps and figures are described below. A rich variety of Csárdás tunes is to be found in dance albums.

CSÁRDÁS STEPS

(Time signature 4/4)

BASIC STEP

Step forward or sideways on l foot.
Close r foot to l foot without changing weight.
Repeat on r foot.
The timing may be varied according to whether a quick or slow step is wanted.

Ornamented

a Step sideways on l foot.
Close r foot to l foot, changing weight.
Step sideways on l foot.
Throw r foot forward and sideways from the knee.
Repeat, beginning on r foot.

b As in *a*, but instead of throwing the leg forward and sideways, click the heels together.
This variation is often danced with a partner, waist and shoulder grasp, with a slight turn to L and R alternately.

c Step sideways on l foot, on the ball.
Close r foot beside l foot, also on the ball.
Click l heel to r heel.
Click r heel to l heel.
Click l heel to r heel.

Repeat, beginning on r foot.

N.B.—The timing of the ' step close ' and the number of heel clicks may be varied.

	Beats
BOKÁZÓ (*Ankling step*). Used as a breakdown at the end of a phrase.	
Man's Step	
Stand in 1st position.	
Raise r heel outward, keeping r toe on the ground.	1
Raise l heel outward, so that the weight is on the balls of both feet with toes turned in.	2
Close heels sharply together.	3
Hold the position on the balls of the feet.	4
Woman's Step	
Stand in 1st position.	
Point r foot forward on the toe.	1
Point l foot forward on the toe.	2
Close heels together with a beat.	3
Hold the position on the balls of the feet.	4
HARANG (*Bell-step*: pas de Bourrée in 1st position)	
Start with r foot raised sideways, toe pointed.	
Close r foot to l foot, changing weight.	1
Step on l foot on the spot.	and
Step on r foot on the spot, pointing l toe sideways.	2 and
Repeat, beginning with l foot.	3 & 4 &

The step is quiet and the body moves in one piece so that the movement resembles the swinging of a pendulum.

HEGYEZŐ (*Heeling or pointing step*)	
Place l foot forward on heel (toe up and out), hopping on r foot.	1
Place l foot forward on toe, hopping on r foot.	2
Repeat on opposite foot.	3–4

This step is danced with partners standing side by side, the man holding his partner on his r arm, her l arm resting on his shoulder. The step is danced on the spot, and the heel and toe movements may be varied.

UGRÓS (*Hopping step*)
Hop on r foot.   1
Hop on r foot, raising l leg sharply upward, knee bent and toe pointing down.   2
Repeat on l foot.   3-4

This step may be danced facing forward or facing partner; in the latter case a turn is made alternately to L and R.

DÜBBENÖS FORDULÓ (*Stamping turn*)
The man holds the woman on his r arm and takes two steps—l, r—making half a turn to the L and swinging his partner on to his l arm; both dancers spring in the air, stretching the ankles, and land with a strong beat with the heels on the ground, knees well bent.   1-2

                                                                                                              3

Repeat the spring and heel beat.   4
Repeat the whole movement, turning to R.

N.B.—During the heel beats, the man raises his free arm quickly and calls 'hopp-hopp'.

CSAPÁSOLÓ (*Leg-throws*)
Man's step. Swing the legs alternately forward and backward with a rhythmic slapping with one or both hands on the thighs. Legs are changed with a spring at will.

This step is performed by the men alone at the start of the dance. As they dance, they call out the name of the girl they would like as a partner. She approaches them with Bokázó step.

PALÓC MÁRTOGATÓS VAGY KUKORGÓS

(Dipping or Squatting Dance)

Region   Palóc.

Character   A gay dance characterised by the man lifting the girl.

Formation   Couple dance. Man's hands on woman's waist, her hands on his shoulders.

Dance

The step used throughout is best described as a 'Skid' step, and is slightly different for man and woman.

MAN'S STEP. One foot is moved forward while the other is moved backward into 4th position, most of the weight on the front foot, the back heel just off the floor. The feet are changed with a sliding or skidding action.

WOMAN'S STEP. Start in and maintain a low 1st position (heels together) throughout the step. The feet are moved backward and forward alternately along the ground with a sliding or skidding action, the weight is mainly on the balls of the feet, and there is only very slight movement in each direction.

	MUSIC Bars
6 Skid steps, the man going forward with r foot, the woman moving slightly backward first.	1–3
The man lifts the girl, who jumps as she likes and lands in a low 1st position.	4
5 Skid steps, starting as before.	5–6
Repeat the lift.	7

PALÓC MÁRTOGATÓS

Arranged by Arnold Foster

5 Skid steps, the man starting with 1 foot forward, the woman moving forward first. [Continue to 1st beat of bar 10]	8–9 10 (beat 1)
Repeat the lift. [From 2nd beat of bar 10 to 1st beat of bar 11]	10 (beats 2 & 3) 11 (beat 1)
6 Skid steps, the man starting with 1 foot forward, the woman moving forward first. [From 2nd beat of bar 11 to end]	11–13

Plate 3
Kalotaszeg

KALOTASZEGI FORGÓS (*Turning Dance*)

Region Kalotaszeg.

Character The dance starts quietly and works up into a rhythmical whirling of the woman, controlled by the man.

Formation Couple dance.

Dance	MUSIC *Bars*
Partners face one another. The man holds the woman's r hand in his l hand, fingers interlaced; his r hand is placed below her shoulder-blades, her l hand resting on his r shoulder. The knees are slightly bent throughout the dance, the weight being mainly on the balls of the feet, heels hardly raised.	
STEP 1 8 walking steps turning C to make one complete circle, starting with r foot across.	1–2
STEP 2 8 walking steps continuing to move C but turning twice round.	3–4
STEP 3 16 walking steps (double-time), turning twice round C.	5–6
STEP 4 The man stands firmly with feet apart (2nd position), holding the woman's r	7–8

KALOTASZEGI FORGÓS

Arranged by Arnold Foster

hand in his r hand and whirling her round four times C-C under his arm, with a whipping accent at the beginning of each turn. The woman takes 16 small steps during the turns, bending her knees slightly at the beginning of each turn and rising a little during the turns.

N.B.—The four movements are continuous and are not divided into four steps when dancing.

KUNSZENTMIKLÓSI VERBUNKOS (Recruiting Dance)

Region Kunszentmiklós.

Character A lively dance with precise movements and marked pauses.

Formation Eight men in a circle round one man in the centre.

Dance	MUSIC
Throughout the dance hands are placed behind the back, palms outward, except when required for clapping movements.	*Bars*

STEP 1 — A

Click heels together, 4 times to each bar (16 times in all). 1–4

3 heel kicks, clapping hands 3 times and replacing them behind back on 4th beat. 5

Repeat the above movements twice. 1–5 } 6–10

STEP 2 — B

All travel C-C, the centre man taking slightly smaller steps. 11

Short step forward on r foot [beat 1]; click heels together twice [beats 2, 3]; pause with heels together [beat 4].

Repeat 4 times, always starting with r foot with a quick knee bend in 1st position at the beginning of each movement. 12–15

Repeat with l foot, travelling C. 11–15

Repeat with r foot, travelling C-C. 16–20

KUNSZENTMIKLÓSI VERBUNKOS

Arranged by Arnold Foster

STEP 3 | C
Step sideways and slightly forwards on r foot [beat 1]; close l foot to r foot [beat 2]; spring on r foot, swinging l leg across with straight knee [beats 3 and 4]. | 21
The step is made with a slight turn of body and feet to L, making a small semi-circle.

Repeat the step on the l foot, turning to R in small semi-circle. | 22

Repeat on alternate feet six times. | 23–28

N.B.—After the first step the movement works up so that there is a slight spring on the first beat as well as on the third.

STEP 4 | A
All face the centre of the circle.
Click heels together, 4 times to each bar; circle the forearms round one another C-C, twice to each bar, the accent being downward. | 1–4

3 heel clicks; arm movement until beat 3, when the hands are clapped. | 5

Repeat the heel clicks with arm movement. | 1–4

3 heel clicks; circle forearms half round, then clap hands on beats 2 and 3. | 5

Repeat the heel clicks with arm movement. | 6–9

3 heel clicks, clapping the hands 3 times and holding the position for the final beat. | 10

N.B.—Before Step 4 is danced, Steps 1–3 may be repeated at a greater speed. The dance always ends with Step 4 (A music).

KARÁDI BEBUG-VERBUNK (Recruiting Dance)

Region Karád.

Character A bold strong dance, performed with a proud and upright carriage of the body.

Formation A man's solo dance.

Dance

	MUSIC Bars
STEP 1	
4 stamps on the spot, starting with r foot. The arms are held high above the head and the body turns from r to l.	1
3 stamping steps travelling forward, the body facing forward on the fourth beat.	2
2 change-of-steps forward on the balls of the feet in the rhythm 'quick, quick, slow; quick, quick, slow', i.e.: Step forward on l foot. Close r to l in 1st position. Step forward on l foot. Repeat on r foot.	3
Repeat bars 1–3, starting with l foot.	4–6
STEP 2	
Hop eight times on alternate feet, starting on the l foot and slapping the opposite heel which is raised forwards.	7–8
4 stamps on the spot, with knees well bent, in the rhythm 'quick, quick, slow, and slow'. The arms are held sideways during the stamps.	9
Repeat bars 7–9.	10–12

KARÁDI BEBUG-VERBUNK

Arranged by Arnold Foster

PRONUNCIATION

It may be helpful to readers of this book to explain the pronunciation of the Hungarian words used. The Hungarian language, or Magyar, is not in fact as difficult to pronounce as it appears at first sight.

The stress is always on the first syllable.

B, D, F, H, K, L, M, N, P, R, T, V and Z are pronounced as in English.

A is short and rounded, as in 'w*a*tch'; Á is long and pure, as in 'f*a*ther'.

E is short and open, as in 'f*ea*ther'; É is long and closed, roughly as in 'f*a*te'.

I as in 'p*i*t'; O as in 'N*o*vember'; U as in 'p*u*t'. Í, Ó and Ú are the lengthened versions, as in 'gr*ee*n', 'm*o*re', 'm*oo*n'.

Ö is like the French EU in 'd*eu*x'.

Ü is the French U in 'l*u*ne'.

C (formerly also spelt CZ) is like TS in 'bi*ts*'. It is never pronounced K.

CS is the English CH in '*ch*at'.

G is always hard as in '*g*et'.

GY is like the DI in 'sol*di*er'. LY is pronounced as in 'mi*lli*on' (but at the end of a word the L is mute and the Y forms a diphthong with the vowel before: Kodály = *code-eye*). Similarly, NY as in 'mi*ni*on', and TY as in 'be*t y*ou'.

J is the English Y as in '*y*es'.

S is pronounced as the English SH.

SZ is the unvoiced s of '*s*it'.

ZS is the sound of the s in 'mea*s*ure'.

Plate 4
Palóc region

BIBLIOGRAPHY

RÉTHEI PRIKKEL, MARIÁN.—*A Magyarság Táncai.* Budapest, 1924. (Hungarian Dances.)

LAJTHA, LÁSZLÓ, and GÖNYEY, SÁNDOR.— *Tánc.* In: *Magyarság Néprajza* (Hungarian Folklore) vol. IV, Budapest, 1937. (A thorough record of up-to-date research, with photographic and musical illustrations.)

VISKI, KÁROLY.—*Hungarian Dances.* Budapest and London, 1937.

REARICK, ELIZABETH C.—*Dances of the Hungarians.* New York, 1939.

BOGYÓ, GEORGIE.—*Six Simple Hungarian Dances.* London, 1941. (A brief description of steps, and some recreational dances, composed by the author.)

LUGOSSY, EMMA, and GÖNYEY, SÁNDOR.—*Magyar Népi Táncok.* Budapest, 1947. (15 Couple dances described in Hungarian text and Lábán-Knust dance-scores.)

MOLNÁR, ISTVÁN.—*Magyar Tánchagyományok.* Budapest, 1947. (With illustrations recording folk dances from documentary films.)

GUNDA, BÉLA (Ed.).—*Kodály Emlékkönyv.* Budapest, 1942. (Contributions by Hungarian and foreign experts on dances and music, summarised in English, French or German.)

TÁLASI, ISTVÁN.—*A Magyar Táncokról.* Budapest, 1949. (On Hungarian Dances.)

BARTÓK, BÉLA.—*A Magyar Népdal.* Budapest, 1924. (A fundamental work on Hungarian folk songs, containing 320 melodies. Translated by M. D. Calvocoressi as *Hungarian Folk Music*, Oxford, 1931.)

KODÁLY, ZOLTÁN.—*Zene.* In: *Magyarság Néprajza*, vol. IV, Budapest, 1937. (An authoritative study of Hungarian folk music, by its greatest expert.)

SZABOLCSI, BENCE.—*A Magyar Zenetörténet Kézikönyve.* Budapest, 1947. (History of Hungarian Music.)

ORTUTAY, GYULA.—*A Magyar Népmüveszét.* 2 vols. Budapest, 1940. (Hungarian Folk Art.)

DOCUMENTARY FILMS: 16 mm. silent films, showing dancing in 33 villages in all parts of the country, are in the archives of the Ethnological Department, East European Institute, Budapest, and of six other villages in those of the Ethnographical Museum.

www.ingramcontent.com/pod-product-compliance
Lightning Source LLC
Chambersburg PA
CBHW061743290426
43661CB00127B/969